JOURNAL with ME

Mother/Daughter
Devotional Study on
PHILIPPIANS 4:4-9

Preteen & Teen Girls

Weekly Conversations With You And Your Girl

By Annie Pajcic

THOUARTEXALTED

Creating Art through God's Word

www.thouartexalted.com

JOURNAL WITH ME • *Mother/Daughter Devotional Study for Preteen and Teen Girls on Philippians 4:4-9*
Text copyright © 2013 by Annie Pajcic
Published by Annie Pajcic Design, Jacksonville, Florida

ISBN-13: 978-0-9896141-1-5
ISBN-10: 0-9896141-1-5

Art Direction, Interior Composition, and Design, by Annie Pajcic © 2013.
Printed in the United States of America
www.thouartexalted.com

THIS BOOK BELONGS TO: _Liya Gilbert_ AND _Kyra Gilbert_

DATE: _October 14, 2018_

As a Mom of two girls and two boys, I know how BUSY life can be. It is only in the purposeful times of **slowing down** and studying God's Word that we discover the amazing truths He has for us. Life is hard, and we need to be equipped for the challenges ahead. *Journal with Me* is an **excellent** way to start. What could be better than studying God's Word as a mother/daughter team?

JOURNAL with ME is a **devotional/study** through **six verses** in Philippians designed especially for mothers with preteen and teenage daughters. Whether you choose to use this study weekly or every two-weeks, each lesson will focus on **one verse**. *JOURNAL with ME* is designed for you to grow in God's Word AND grow deeper in your relationship together.

Here's how it works:

*1. Find a favorite **place** and **time** to meet. This meeting spot could be your favorite coffee shop, a local breakfast cafe, or even your own home. The important part is to make this a special place for the **two of you**. You will need to schedule at least 30-45 minutes of time.*

*2. Bring **Journal with Me**, a Bible, and a pen.*

*3. Complete the first lesson and answer the questions together. Take turns reading, and always begin by reading **Philippians 4:4-9**.*

*4. During the week, pass the journal back and forth to answer the "journal time" questions. Each chapter is divided into five lessons: One lesson with each other and four lessons to be done individually. Both are designed to be **special** times to write down your thoughts and begin building a lifelong relationship together. Each chapter also includes: **a challenge**, **a memory verse**, and **an art project or service idea** to experience together.*

5. When you have completed the chapter, meet again at your "special spot" and begin the next lesson.

A note for: MOMS

I always treasure the conversations I have with my girls, especially those concerning real-life issues. Life gets tricky as they get older and watching them apply God's Word to their lives is a blessing. *Journal with Me* is a not only a devotional/journal, but also a "keepsake" of memories. Prayerfully, you can look back into your *Journal with Me* and see the hand of God as He carries you through your circumstances, answers your prayers, and equips you and your daughter to shine for His glory in this adventure called **life.**

A note for: DAUGHTERS

Have you ever wondered what your Mom was like when she was your age? Have you ever wanted to ask her questions but didn't know how to get started? You can now! You and your Mom will pick out a **special** place to meet. Using your *Journal with Me*, you will study the Bible together and answer the questions during the week. You will also get the opportunity to make some really cool art, memorize scripture, and do a service project together. Take your time and start building a special **one-on-one** relationship with your MOM! Remember, she was once your age, too!

On that note, let's get started! Remember to PRAY FOR EACH other as I am praying for you!
With love and blessings,
Annie

"*Rejoice* in the Lord,
I will say it again!
Rejoice!

Philippians 4:4

• **Begin by reading Philippians 4:4-9.**

I can think of no better way to begin *Journal with Me* than to start with Philippians 4:4. *"Rejoice in the Lord, I will say it again! REJOICE!"* I pray that you and your Mom are REJOICING today, because not only are you studying God's Word together, but you have also chosen a really great spot to meet each week. (Hopefully it involves a cafe latte and your favorite breakfast food!)

Opening DISCUSSION

• **When hear the word, REJOICE, what is the first thing you think about? Was it the present you got for Christmas? Was it that championship season? What about the new clothes you just bought, your amazing math grade, or your new friend?**

• **Without looking, what do you think is the definition of REJOICE?**

Definition: REJOICE

to rejoice, to be glad, to rejoice exceedingly, to be well, to give one greetings, joy, joyful. feel or show great joy or delight, be pleased as punch, be on top of the world, over the moon, delirious . . . [1]

The definition of REJOICE can mean many things. Which one is your favorite? I personally liked "pleased as punch!" When we look at the definition in the context of our passage, we discover that rejoicing means to be **exceedingly joyful.** If we look even **deeper** into this passage, we find that the one who is telling us to be JOYFUL is in prison! The apostle Paul was under "house arrest" because of his faith in Jesus. House arrest simply means that Paul was not allowed to leave his house in Rome, however, he could still be involved in his ministry by writing letters to encourage believers in Jesus. Philippians is a letter written by Paul "to strengthen them (the people living in Philippi) in the **hope** and **joy** that was theirs in Christ."[2]

Paul's faith shows us that we can **rejoice always** even when life is not going the way we planned. Why? Rejoicing is a **choice** we make and here's the key (and a quick English lesson). Rejoice is a transitive verb. This means the verb is only complete with a **direct object.** What is the direct object in this verse? You got it! It's the LORD. Although it's good to rejoice in many things, the **key** to rejoicing in ALL things is to make the LORD the direct OBJECT of our joy.

QUESTIONS TOGETHER

1. What makes you happy?

being with family, reading the bible

2. When have you found it hard to be joyful?

when you're mad, stressed, or tired

3. Who is the direct object of your joy (be honest)? What happens when the things that make you "happy" become the object of your joy? Why is it important to have God as the object of your JOY?

we center our joy in God because his love is constant and never ending, we depend on him forever

Always be FULL
of *joy*
in the Lord,
I say it again!

Philippians 4:4 (NLT)

Did you KNOW?

Did you know there is a difference between being **joyful** and being **happy**? Being "happy" depends upon your "happen-ings" or your circumstances. For example, I am HAPPY because my awesome Mom took me to breakfast this morning. I am not happy this morning because my dog slobbered on my report, and I couldn't find my favorite shoes. REJOICING is not dependent on what is happening around you. We can be FULL of JOY, even when we don't feel happy, because our JOY is deeply rooted in God's promises—NOT in our circumstances.

- **What is the difference between being "happy" and being "joyful?"**

Scripture Search

Is it possible to "**ALWAYS** be FULL of Joy in the Lord" (Philippians 4:4)? It's **only** possible when you CHOOSE to be JOYFUL. It's easy to get upset when your plans don't work out, isn't it? It's easy to fall into "pity parties." Notice what the verse says, "Rejoice IN the **LORD**." He is the **object** of our rejoicing. When life gets difficult, **choose** to believe God has a reason for all things. You have a reason to be **joyful** because you KNOW God has a GOOD plan for you. He promises to be near to you. He is a relational God, and He has called you by name.

- **Have you ever felt like God didn't care? Read Jeremiah 29:11.**
What is God's promise for you? How can YOU rejoice even when life is difficult?

> God has a plan for you, to prosper you, give you hope & a future. Thinking good thoughts, taking comfort knowing God has a plan four our lives.

- **What promises are found in Isaiah 43:2-3?**
Underline the words that are most important to you in this passage.

> He will redeem, protect us, he will be with us. He is our personal God

"Don't be afraid, I've redeemed you.
I've called your name. You're mine.
When you're in over your head, I'll be there with you.
When you're in rough waters, you will not go down.
When you're between a rock and a hard place,
it won't be a dead end—
Because I am God, your personal God,
The Holy of Israel, your Savior."
Isaiah 43:2-3 (MSG)

Are you going to be afraid when life becomes difficult, or are you going to find **strength** in the LORD? **We can REJOICE always** because His love for us will never change. His love for us will never be taken away. He will always be there for us. THIS is a promise worth rejoicing!

• **Can anything separate you from God's love? Read Romans 8:35, 37-38 from the New Living Translation.**

> "Can anything ever separate us from Christ's love?
> Does it mean he no longer loves us if we have trouble or
> calamity, or are persecuted, or hungry,
> or destitute, or in danger, or threatened with death?
> No, despite all these things, **overwhelming victory**
> is ours through Christ, who loved us.
> And I am convinced that **nothing** can ever separate us from
> God's love. Neither death nor life, neither angels nor demons,
> neither our fears for today nor our worries about tomorrow
> —not even the powers of hell can separate us from God's love."

• **What truth does this verse reveal about God's love? Is this promise true when we are going through a difficult time?**

Yes, nothing separates us from God's love

We will have trouble in this world—it's guaranteed. But, we can REJOICE because we **know** nothing can separate us from God's love. Rejoicing is an **attitude** of our heart. We cannot control our circumstances, but we CAN control the way we respond to them. Let's put our HOPE in Jesus and REJOICE in ALL things. The **overwhelming victory** is ours!

Main Lessons:

1. God needs to be the **DIRECT OBJECT** of your JOY.
2. Happiness depends on your circumstances.
   Joy depends on your choice to **trust** in God.
3. God has a **PLAN** for you, and it is GOOD.
4. God has called you by name and is **ALWAYS** with YOU.
5. NOTHING can separate you from God's **love** through Jesus.

Prayer: ♥

Thank you Lord for this sweet time together. We pray we would learn the meaning of REJOICING in YOU in ALL things. Please give us Your Spirit of JOY, even when life turns upside down. We know YOU have a plan, YOU are with us, and YOU will never leave us. Nothing can separate us from Your love. Strengthen us to REJOICE in You—always. Amen.

SNEAK PEEK:

The week, we will journal about:
- Rejoicing IN the Lord
- Rejoicing as a GREETING
- Rejoicing in our SUFFERING
- Rejoicing as a RESPONSE
- Rejoicing worth REPEATING

JOURNAL TIP:

- What do you do when you have a hard day and don't feel like rejoicing? I like to write down my **blessings**. From the ability to breathe, smile, and eat, to the house I live in, my health, my friends, and my family. What are you thankful for today?

- **Write down the Top TEN BLESSINGS in YOUR life. Discuss why these are special.**

♥ MOMS

1. Our Family
2. Sisters, cousins, friends
3. God,
4. Security, good jobs
5. good health
6. Safety
7. Prosperity
8.
9.
10.

♥ DAUGHTERS

1. Family
2. God
3. Love
4. house
5. talents/gifts
6. good health
7. food
8. experiences
9. everyone around me
10. everything I have

Prayer Requests: date: _____

God to watch over everyone

"Keep on *Rejoicing* in the LORD at *all* times. I will say it again: KEEP on *Rejoicing!*"

Philippians 4:4 (ISV)

• Name ONE person in your life that makes you feel REALLY special. How does this person GREET you when they see you?

Mommy—she hugs me every morning
Daddy—he tells me how much he loves me ..
Luya & Kaden — give me hugs

• Rejoicing is also a way to GREET one another. Read Matthew 28:1-9. How did Jesus "greet" Mary and Mary Magdalene? What do you think their reaction was to see Jesus alive? How were they REJOICING in Him?

He said "Greetings". Mary and Mary Magdalene got on their knees, grasped his feet and worshipped him.

- **Have you ever felt "invisible?" Describe a time in your life when you felt lonely.**

*yes.. living in New York I didn't
know a lot of people
Liya = NO*

> "This is
>
> the
>
> the LORD has MADE;
>
> Let us
>
> and be
>
> in it."
>
> Psalm 118:24
>
> (NASB)

A pastor once told me that when we enter into a room, instead of saying, "Here I am," we should say, "There you are!" When we wake up every morning, we should hear Jesus saying, ___*Liya, Kyra*___ (put your names in the blank), "GREETINGS, REJOICE. There YOU are!" *The Message* says, "Good morning!" You are not invisible to God. Jesus meets you in your troubles, and He meets you in your triumphs. He sees you and invites you to REJOICE in Him. Just as He greeted the two Mary's, He greets us in the same way. There is not one day that goes by that we are not recognized by Him.

- **Jesus greets us this way every day. How are we going to GREET others, REJOICING and being GLAD in it?**

We should say "There you are," instead of "Here I am"

- *Extra Challenge*: MEMORIZE Psalm 118:24. Share with each other how you REJOICED in the Lord!

1 Thessalonians 5:16-18 says:

> "Rejoice always, pray continually, give thanks in all circumstances; for this is God's will for you in Christ Jesus."

• **What are the three things we need to DO for God's will to be accomplished in our lives?**

1. Rejoice always
2. pray continually
3. give thanks in all circumstances

• **God wants you to REJOICE even when you are going through difficult times. Can you remember a time in your life that was difficult? Looking back, did you trust in God and rejoice, or did you pout and blame others? How can you use these three principles of REJOICING, PRAYING, and being THANKFUL to help you the next time you go through a hard time?**

Liya= When I didn't get picked as Dorothy in the play/when I didn't get student council president.

When I didn't get a job offer from Colgate but eventually received job offers from better companies.

> "You know you are living a grateful life when WHATEVER happens is received with an invitation to deepen your heart, to strengthen your love, and to broaden your hope."—Henry Nouwen[3]

Believe there is a PURPOSE to your PROBLEMS. Your TRIALS in life are to teach you to TRUST Him more! Be joyful ALWAYS. **How are you going to do this today?**

• Has your tongue ever gotten you into trouble? Describe a time when your words got the best of you.

yes, mom tends to yell too much!

Liya - I got mad at Siena for not waiting for me at lunch, and I regretted it because she was mad

Rejoicing is a **RESPONSE,** not a REACTION. What do I mean by this? Remember, rejoicing is a **choice** you make because God is the object of your JOY, and not your situation. God tells us to be joyful always, but He never says it's going to be easy. In fact, it's a tough job—especially when someone hurts your feelings! Jesus tells us that when we are weak, He makes us strong. The next time you are "hot-headed" and want to react with unkind words, remember to take a deep breath and respond with Christ's love and in His strength.

• **What does Nehemiah 8:10 tell us about God's STRENGTH? How will this verse help you the next time you want to blurt out words that maybe you should not? Who and what is your strength?**

"That's why I take
pleasure in my
_____ and in the
insults, hardships,
persecutions, and
troubles that I suffer for
Christ. For when
I am weak, then I
am _____."

2 Corinthians 12:10 (NLT)

" . . . the JOY of the LORD is your STRENGTH."
Nehemiah 8:10

Nehemiah 8:10 says that the Joy of the LORD is our strength.

_____
_____
_____
_____
_____

The LORD is the object of our JOY and REJOICING! The next time you are tempted to say words you might regret later, say this prayer:

"For I can do EVERYTHING through Christ, who gives me STRENGTH."
Philippians 4:13 (NLT)

EXTRA *Rejoicing*

• Read John 15:11-13.

Jesus illustrates our relationship with God in John 15. God is the Gardener, Jesus is the True Vine, and we are the branches. When we are attached to the Vine, we are allowing Jesus' strength to flow through us. If we break off from the Vine, this strength is cut off. Jesus tells us this because our JOY is **only** COMPLETE when we are attached to Him. Remember, REJOICING is a transitive verb and is incomplete without a direct object. We, too, are incomplete if we are not directly connected to Jesus. Apart from Him, we can do **nothing.** We are COMPLETE when HE is the object of our strength and JOY.

• **Can you give an example of a decision you made relying on the strength of Jesus. Can you recall a time when you made a decision trusting in your own strength? What is the difference?**

_____
_____
_____
_____
_____
_____
_____
_____
_____
_____
_____
_____
_____
_____

Are you involved in sports? Do you play a musical instrument? Do you have a big test for which you are preparing? Whether it is practice, rehearsal, or studying, why is **repetition** so important?

• In what area of your life are you using REPETITION to strengthen your skills?

Mom- I run regularly & exercise to stay healthy. If I am presenting information for work, I practice several times.

Liya- I practice soccer drills a lot. I practice violin a lot too. I am prepping for the "End of Unit" math test coming up soon.

DAUGHTER

Just like sports or school work, REJOICING takes PRACTICE. The more we CHOOSE to REJOICE, the better we will get! Read Philippians 4:9 and James 1:22-25.

"Keep putting into **practice** all you learned and received from me
--everything you heard from me and saw me doing. Then the God of peace
will be with you." Philippians 4:9 (NLT)

"Do not merely listen to the word, and so deceive yourselves.
Do what it says. Anyone who listens to the word but does not do what it
says is like someone who looks at his face in a mirror and, after looking
at himself, goes away and immediately forgets what he looks like.
But whoever looks intently into the perfect law that gives freedom,
and continues in it—not forgetting what they have heard,
but doing it—they will be **BLESSED** in what they do." James 1:22-25

• **Why do you think it is important to "put into practice" what we learn in the Bible? What happens when we forget what we have heard?**

Then the words became empty if we don't apply it.

We need to put into practice what we learn so that we can remember GOD's word and spread it to others who don't yet know about the word of GOD. When we forget, we cannot share what we learn.

• **Can you name some principles you have put into practice this week? What have you learned this week about REJOICING in the Lord?**

I'm learning it's a choice to rejoice and even when it's hard we need to find joy.

I have learned to rejoice when I am not feeling well, am sad, or I have hurt ~~feeling~~ feelings.

" of the same thought or physical action develops into a which, repeated frequently enough, becomes an automatic ."
Norman Vincent Peale[4]

REJOICING is worth repeating because God's PEACE will be with you, and you will be BLESSED in ALL you do! Read the quote from Norman Vincent Peale. Do you think REJOICING can be an automatic REFLEX?

CHALLENGE: Next time it seems hard to REJOICE, ask GOD to give you strength to fill you with HIS JOY!

MEMORIZE: Go to page 63. Cut and copy the memory verse for this lesson. Post it in your room, tape it to the refrigerator, or take it to school. When you meet together, see if you can say the verse without looking!

ART PROJECT: *Prayer Cards* (Instructions on page 15)

"Rejoice in the Lord, I will say it again!

Philippians 4:4

PRAYER CARD

PRAYER REQUESTS:

Place your picture here.

date:

ART SUPPLIES:

- Copier/ Card Stock
- Picture of YOU
- Pen
- Scissors
- Glue stick
- Laminate or contact paper (Optional)

ART INSTRUCTIONS:

• It's simple! You can either use the template I have provided, or you can make your own prayer card from an index card using cute scrapbook paper to decorate. 1. Take a picture of yourself and glue it onto the card. 2. Write down the date and your prayer requests. 3. For protection, laminate or wrap your card in contact paper. 4. Swap prayer cards, and remember to pray for each other every day!

- **Open with prayer and ask God to be with you in your time together.**

- **Take five minutes to discuss last week's** *Journal with Me.* **What did you learn? How did you make your joy COMPLETE by rejoicing in the Lord?**

- **Start by reading Philippians 4:4-9.**

"Let your gentleness be evident to ALL. THE *Lord is near."*
Philippians 4:5

Opening DISCUSSION

In this lesson, we will study Philippians 4:5.

"Let your gentleness be evident to all. The Lord is near."

- **There are THREE key words in this verse. What do you think they are?**

1. _____ 2. _____ 3. _____

> **Definition: GENTLENESS**
> considerate, kind or tender in behavior, not harsh or severe, mild and soft, easily managed, sensitivity of disposition and kindness of behavior, founded on strength and prompted by love. [1]

If you answered **gentleness, evident**, and **near**, you are right! We will study these words in detail this week and learn how they are woven together with the golden thread of God's love.

- **Before reading the definition of gentleness, what do you think it means?**

_____

_____

_____

_____

_____

In the Bible, gentleness can refer to **many** things. Gentleness can be connected to our speech and also how we respond (not react) to people. Gentleness is a fruit of the Spirit and is also used to describe the character of Jesus.

In the last lesson, we learned that we are called to **REJOICE in the Lord**—repeatedly. This lesson, we are called to follow another action: *"Let our gentleness be evident to ALL . . ."* (Philippians 4:5). Let's focus on the word **evidence**. Evidence means: *"the available information indicating whether a belief or proposition is true."* [2] Simply stated, evidence is **proof** of something. Paul is telling us in verse five that our gentleness is **proof** of our faith in God. What do I mean by evidence? Let's say your room is really messy, but when you come home from school, it's all CLEAN! How do you know someone cleaned your room? It's simple—the EVIDENCE. There are no clothes on the floor, your bed is made, and your drawers are shut. WOW. I bet you wish this would happen everyday!

• **Philippians 4:5 says that our gentleness should be EVIDENT. What are ways our gentleness can be evident?**

_____

_____

_____

• **Name someone in your life who has the characteristic of gentleness. What is the EVIDENCE or proof of their gentleness?**

_____

_____

_____

_____

Did you KNOW? Before Christ was born, the prophet Zechariah predicted that Jesus would be **gentle.** *"See, your king comes to you, righteous and having salvation, gentle and riding on a donkey, on a colt, the foal of a donkey"* (Zechariah 9:9). **Five hundred years** after the prophesy of Zechariah, Jesus entered Jerusalem riding on a donkey on the Christian holiday we now call Palm Sunday. Scripture tells us:

```
"The disciples . . . brought the donkey and the colt, placed their cloaks on them, and
   Jesus sat on them. A very large crowd spread their cloaks on the road, while others
cut branches from the trees and spread them on the road. The crowds went ahead of him
          and shouted . . . 'Blessed is He who comes in the name of the Lord!
                     Hosanna in the highest!'" (Matthew 21:6-9)
```

Scripture Search

One of Jesus' many characteristics is **gentleness**—kindness, tenderness, and consideration toward others. Jesus did not show favoritism. He showed gentleness to **ALL**. Regardless of age, gender, or power, Jesus healed the sick, the hurting, and the poor. Read the following verses and find the EVIDENCE of His gentle touch.

• **Read Mark 1:40-42.**
Whom did Jesus heal? Why do you think Jesus was filled with compassion?

_____

_____

_____

Do you know about **leprosy**? It is a contagious disease that "affects the skin and nerves, causing discoloration and lumps on the skin and, in severe cases, disfigurement and deformities."[3] According to Jewish law, touching a man who was leprous would make that person "unclean"—not able to worship God. Despite this, Jesus reached out and touched this man. He healed his disease and his heart that was so deeply hurt from being an outcast.

• Read Mark 10:13-16.
Whom did Jesus place on His lap? What action of gentleness did Jesus take?
Why do you think this was significant?

_____

_____

_____

_____

Children were also considered to be insignificant in the days of Jesus. The Scriptural evidence proves two things. First, the disciples were trying to get rid of the children. Second, Jesus was angry at the disciple's behavior. Jesus **proves** His love for the little children when He **INVITES** them to come to Him and jump in His lap to BLESS them.

• Read Matthew 11:28-29.
Who was Jesus asking to come to Him? What does He promise those who come?
How does Jesus describe Himself?

_____

_____

_____

_____

Jesus came to heal and show His gentleness to **ALL** of us. Ephesians 5:1 tell us to _"imitate God"_ (NLT). Philippians 4:5 is inviting us to follow Jesus' example and copy His actions, allowing our gentleness to be visible to all. Why? He wants us to be an example of His love to others.

```
  "Imitate God, therefore, in everything you do, because you are his dear children.
     Live a life filled with love, following the example of Christ. He loved us and
  offered himself as a sacrifice for us, a pleasing aroma to God." Ephesians 5:1,2 (NLT)
```

To imitate means to copy. Drawing from the verses you have just read, how can you **imitate the love of Jesus** this week—making your gentleness known to all? Is there someone specific with whom you need to show God's gentleness?

By showing gentleness to all, we are showing others the love of God. **Gentleness is the EVIDENCE of God's love.**

Main Lessons:

```
• Let your gentleness be evident to ALL.
• Your gentleness shows others that you love God.
• Evidence is proof of your actions.
```

Prayer: ♥

Lord, thank You for this special time together. You show us by example that You want us to demonstrate gentleness to others. You healed lepers. You touched children. You tell us to come to YOU when we are weary and tired. You offer us rest. Help us this week to imitate YOU and prove our gentleness to others. We desire to glorify You in our actions. We pray that we are living PROOF of Your love. Amen.

SNEAK PEEK:

This week, we will journal about:
- Gentle Action
- Gentle Shepherd
- Gentle Words
- Gentle Spirit
- Gentle Evidence

"Let everyone see that you are considerate in ALL you do. REMEMBER, THE Lord is coming soon.

Philippians 4:5 (NLT)

• Write down the Top TEN BEST GIFTS you have ever received. Discuss why these were special?

♥ MOMS

1. _____
2. _____
3. _____
4. _____
5. _____
6. _____
7. _____
8. _____
9. _____
10. _____

♥ DAUGHTERS

1. _____
2. _____
3. _____
4. _____
5. _____
6. _____
7. _____
8. _____
9. _____
10. _____

Prayer Requests: date: _____

"Let your gentle spirit be KNOWN to ALL men. THE *Lord is near."*

Philippians 4:5 (NASB)

• **Begin today by reading the different translations of Isaiah 40:11.**

> "He will feed his flock like a shepherd. He will carry the lambs in his arms, holding them close to his heart. He will gently lead the mother sheep with their young." (NLT)
>
> "He tends his flock like a shepherd. He gathers the lambs in his arms and carries them close to his heart; he gently leads those that have young." (NIV)

• **What are the verbs in these passages? Choose five.**

_____, _____, _____, _____, _____.

(feed, carry, hold, lead, tend, gathers, and carries)

This Old Testament passage is an illustration that points to the **gentleness of Jesus** who came to take care of His people as a **shepherd** takes care of his flock.

• **What evidence of gentleness is shown by the shepherd in this verse? (Isaiah 40:11)**

_____

_____

_____

_____

_____

_____

_____

_____

_____

_____

• **Read John 10:1-11. List the EVIDENCE that the shepherd knows his sheep and the sheep know their shepherd. How is Jesus like this shepherd?**

_____

_____

_____

_____

• **How has Jesus, the Good Shepherd, taken care of you lately?** Just as the little children climbed onto His lap, and received a blessing, how has Jesus called you by name, put His hands on you, and blessed you? (Moms, think of an example when you were your daughter's age.)

JOURNAL TIME: GENTLE *Words*

The Bible teaches us we should be **gentle with our words** and how we should speak to one another. In fact, we will find that being gentle has a lot of POWER. It sounds like the opposite should be true, but it's not!

• **Read Proverbs 15:1.**

> "A gentle answer turns away wrath, but a harsh word stirs up anger."

Have you ever noticed when you get angry, you tend to say words you regret later? What is the evidence of a **gentle answer**? A gentle response turns away our anger. What is the evidence of a cruel word spoken? You got it! Harsh answers only stir up more anger.

God says, *"Be quick to listen, slow to speak and slow to become angry, for man's anger does not bring about the righteous life that God desires"* (James 1:19-20). God desires us to be gentle in our **actions** and in our **speech.**

• **Think of a time when you were really angry. Did you show evidence of a gentle response, or did you react with a harsh answer? Be honest. What was the EVIDENCE that proved your response?**

MOM

DAUGHTER

The next time you find yourself "hot-headed," take a deep breath, and pray for **gentleness** to take control of your tongue. Gentleness has *more power* than an angry reaction.

JOURNAL TIME: GENTLE *Spirit*

• **Today's verse might be familiar to you! Read Galatians 5:22-23.**

> "But the fruit of the Spirit is love, joy, peace, patience, kindness, goodness, faithfulness, GENTLENESS and self-control . . ."

What is the eighth fruit? It's **gentleness.** In our last lesson, we learned a gentle answer can turn away anger. Today, we learn why. It's a **fruit** of the Spirit. Just as an orange is the fruit of an orange tree, gentleness is a fruit of the Spirit. The Bible tells us that the Spirit of God **lives** in us when we believe in Jesus (Romans 8:9-10). The Spirit also **helps** us when we are weak (Romans 8:26) and **counsels** us in truth (John 14:16-17). The Spirit **teaches** us and **reminds** us of what the Bible says (John 14:26). When we have the Spirit, we have the ability to REJOICE despite difficulties. We also have the ability to respond with "love, joy, peace, patience, kindness, goodness, faithfulness, **GENTLENESS,** and self-control."

When we live by the Spirit, we are living **PROOF of God's love.**

• What fruit do you need today? How will this fruit help you through a specific situation in your life?

JOURNAL TIME: GENTLE *Evidence*

• The second part of Philippians 4:5 says, *"The Lord is near."* What do you think this means?

"Let your gentleness be evident to ALL. THE *Lord is near."* Philippians 4:5

Let's imagine your teacher leaves the classroom and puts YOU in charge. She has promised to return, but you have no idea when. What will she find when she comes back? Will she find the class in total disorder? Or, will she find you have risen to the top and done your BEST to keep everything in order and in peace? Before His death on the cross, Jesus told His disciples that He was leaving to return to the Father, but He promised **to return** to get them. This promise is for **all** who believe in His name. Jesus is returning. When He does, will He find you imitating His gentleness?

• **Read the following verses.**

> "I am the way, the truth and the life. No one comes to the Father except through me." John 14:6
>
> "For God so loved _____(replace your name for "the world") that He give His one and only son that whoever believes in Him will not perish but have eternal life." John 3:16

• **What do these verses mean to you?**

_____

_____

_____

_____

_____

_____

_____

_____

_____

_____

_____

_____

_____

_____

_____

CHALLENGE: How are you going to show your GENTLENESS to ALL this week? Can you PROVE it?

MEMORIZE: Go to page 63. Cut and copy the memory verse for this week. Remember to post it somewhere you can read it everyday! When you are with each other, see if you can say it!

SERVICE PROJECT: Show your GENTLENESS this week by **baking cookies** for your teacher, making a **flower arrangement** for someone in need, or making a **card** for someone who is sick. Let's PROVE God's love today!

Lesson THREE: *Prayer!*

- **Open with prayer and ask God to be with you in your time together.**

- **Take five minutes to discuss last week's *Journal with Me*. What did you learn? What did you learn about proving your gentleness? Why should it be evident to all?**

- **Start by reading Philippians 4:4-9.**

Opening DISCUSSION

In this lesson, we will study Philippians 4:6.

"Do not be anxious about anything, but in every situation, by prayer and petition, with thanksgiving, present your requests to God."

- **What is the ONE thing Philippians 4:6 tells us NOT to do?** _____

- **What are the THREE things this verse tells us TO do?** _____, be _____, and _____

"Do not be anxious about anything, but in every situation, by prayer and petition, with thanksgiving, present your requests to God" Philippians 4:6

Definition: WORRY

allow one's mind to dwell on difficulty or troubles, a state of anxiety and uncertainty over actual or potential problems [1]

God teaches us **three ways** to overcome worry. He is not a God that simply says, "Don't do it." He gives us practical solutions to help us when worry creeps into our lives.

- **Before reading the definition of WORRY, what do you think it means?**

_____

_____

The last two lessons taught us two things: **REJOICE always** (even when life is hard), and **let our gentle spirits be evident to everyone.** Both rejoicing and gentleness are **PROOF** of our love for God. Today, we learn the **one thing** that steals our rejoicing and our gentle spirits. It's a five letter word called W-O-R-R-Y. Worry, also called anxiety, steals our joy because we focus upon our difficulty and not upon God. Have you ever seen a horse race? Race horses wear "blinders" beside their eyes to help them stay focused on one thing—the track ahead. Horses, like us, get easily distracted from what is most important. Paul tells us plain and simple, "DO NOT WORRY about ANYTHING." And anything covers **everything**! Don't get distracted. Keep your focus upon God.

QUESTIONS TOGETHER

What are three things you are worried about today?
1. _____
2. _____
3. _____

We worry about everything, don't we? We worry about the weather, tests, friendships, grades, and sports. We worry about what people think about us, our families, and our clothes. We ask questions like, "Will I be invited to THAT party?" and "What will they think of my haircut?" Why do we worry so much? Has worry ever **added** anything to your life? Have you ever accomplished anything by worrying? Worry doesn't move us forward. It only moves us **backwards**. Have you ever played the game "Chutes and Ladders?" Worry is like a chute. We can be focused on winning the game, when we hit the slide that takes us all the way back to the beginning. Worry takes the joy right out of the word *joy-ful*. Bummer.

"Worry does not empty tomorrow of its sorrow; it only empties TODAY of its strength."
Corrie ten Boom [2]

Scripture Search

What does Jesus tell us about worry? He must think it's an important lesson for us to learn because He dedicates **10 verses** to teach us about it. Let's find out why.

- **Start by reading Matthew 6:25-27.**
- **What is more important than food or clothes? Why?**

_____

_____

_____

_____

- **What does this story teach us about worry? Who is taking care of us?**

_____

_____

_____

Why do we worry about food and clothes?

Jesus is reminding us that **we** are more loved than the birds in the air of whom the Father takes COMPLETE care. Do YOU BELIEVE God takes care of you in this way—completely? Do you really think by worrying you can add an hour to your life? Sounds simple, doesn't it? So, why is it so hard?

- **Read Matthew 6:28-34.**
- **What does Jesus say about the lilies of the field which are here today and gone tomorrow?**

_____

_____

_____

- **Knowing the magnitude of God's love and the completeness of His care, how should we act?**

_____

_____

• **What is the key verse in this passage? (I'll give you a hint: Matthew 6:33.)**
Write this verse below.

_____

_____

_____

• **What do you think it means TO SEEK His Kingdom first? Where should we go BEFORE we start to worry?**

_____

_____

_____

• **What are the "things" in this verse God is talking about? (Matthew 6:30)**

_____

_____

_____

• **Why shouldn't we worry about tomorrow? What is promised for tomorrow? (Matthew 6:34)**

_____

_____

_____

In our last lesson, we studied how **gentleness** is the EVIDENCE of our faith in God. This week, we learn that WORRY is PROOF we do NOT TRUST in God completely. Instead of seeking God's counsel first and believing in His perfect plan for our lives, we are telling God that we want to be in control. Do you really think that by worrying, you are gaining more control? God loves you FAR MORE than you could ever imagine, and He created you with a special purpose in mind. He tells you to TRUST in Him because He's got EVERYTHING under control. E-V-E-R-Y-thing! When you start to worry this week, repeat these words: **God's got EVERYTHING under control. I pray to seek Your advice FIRST, and I do not have to worry about anything.** In our journal time together, we will discover ways to let go of WORRY and to TRUST more in God.

Main Lessons:

• God tells us NOT to WORRY about ANYTHING.
• Worry is proof that we do not trust in God.
• When we SEEK HIM FIRST, all things shall be added to us.

Prayer: ♥

Lord, thank You for this special time together. Worrying is so easy. We can worry about the smallest detail in our lives and also about what tomorrow will bring. Help us to believe YOU have ALL the details under Your control. You will take care of us like the birds in the air and the lilies in the field. We cannot gain another day by worrying about something. Teach us to let go of our worry and TRUST more in YOU! Amen.

SNEAK PEEK:

This week, we will journal about:
- NOT WORRYING
- WORRY as a THIEF
- PRAYER WARRIORS
- THANKSGIVING
- GIVING it to GOD

"Don't worry about anything; instead, pray about everything. Tell God what you NEED, and thank Him for all He has done."

Philippians 4:6 (NLT)

• **Write down your Top TEN Favorite FOODS. Discuss why these are special.**

♥ MOMS

1. _____
2. _____
3. _____
4. _____
5. _____
6. _____
7. _____
8. _____
9. _____
10. _____

♥ DAUGHTERS

1. _____
2. _____
3. _____
4. _____
5. _____
6. _____
7. _____
8. _____
9. _____
10. _____

Prayer Requests: date: _____

JOURNAL TIME: Worry as a *Thief*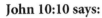

JOURNAL TIP:
• Don't WORRY about ANYTHING! That means EVERYTHING! What are you going to trust God for today?

• **Begin today by reading the New Living Translation of Philippians 4:6.**

> "Don't worry about anything; instead, pray about everything. Tell God what you NEED, and thank HIM for all He has done."

John 10:10 says:

"The thief comes only to steal and kill and destroy; I have come that they may have life, and have it to the full."

• **How would you describe a thief? What do they want?**

_____

_____

_____

_____

_____

_____

_____

_____

_____

_____

_____

_____

Thieves are selfish and only want what they do not HAVE. Worry is just like this! **Worry** is the thief that comes to steal your joy in the Lord. God has promised you that if you SEEK HIM **first**, you will have EVERYTHING you NEED in this life. You do not **have** to worry about anything. Read the New Living Translation of Matthew 6:33.

> "Seek the Kingdom of God above all else, and live righteously, and he will give you everything you need."

• **What do you think it means to live righteously?**

_____

_____

_____

_____

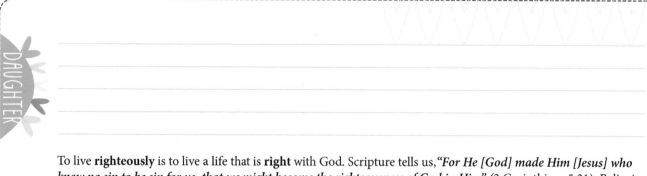

To live **righteously** is to live a life that is **right** with God. Scripture tells us, *"For He [God] made Him [Jesus] who knew no sin to be sin for us, that we might become the righteousness of God in Him"* (2 Corinthians 5:21). Believing the **perfect** life of Jesus was given for our **imperfect** lives, puts us into a **right** relationship with God. Righteous living is being obedient to God's commands and giving up the control of WORRY. It is TRUSTING to let God take charge.

JOURNAL TIME: PRAYER *Warriors*

Philippians 4:6 tells us not only to give up WORRY, but also **HOW** to do it! I love this about God. He doesn't just say, "Do not worry," but gives us the tools to help us. **PRAYER** is the first tool to get rid of WORRY.

John 14:1 says:

> "Don't let your hearts be troubled.
> Trust in God, and trust also in me." (NLT)

A troubled heart is a worried heart. What does God say to do? Yes, TRUST in HIM.

• **What do you need to trust God for in your life? How are you going to do this?**

Philippians 4:6 tells us to PRAY about everything! Just as a "bomb squad" diffuses bombs, prayer will diffuse WORRY. God cares about us and wants us to believe and trust in Him. Give Him your worry today!

• **Read 1 Peter 5:7.**

> "Give all your worries and cares to God, for he cares about you."
> 1 Peter 5:7 (NLT)

Another TOOL to help us diffuse WORRY is being THANKFUL! The definition of being thankful is: "expressing gratitude and relief."[3]

• **How does being thankful relieve us from worry?**

_____
_____
_____
_____
_____
_____
_____
_____
_____
_____
_____

• **What are you worried about today? What specific thanksgivings can be made to "diffuse" your worry?**

WORRY: _____
_____
_____

THANKSGIVING: _____
_____
_____

WORRY: _____
_____
_____

THANKSGIVING: _____
_____
_____

Let's review our verse for this lesson.

> *"Do not be anxious about anything, but in every situation,*
> *by prayer and petition, with thanksgiving,*
> *present your requests to God." Philippians 4:6*

Fill in the blanks:

Do not _____ about ANYTHING. _____ about EVERYTHING.

Tell God what you need and be _____.

Key: **Worry, Pray, Thankful** (I sure hope you got an A+ on our little test!)

God cares about your life, and He wants you to tell Him everything. Take, for example, your friendships. Your best friendships are built upon the **time** you spend together and how much you **talk** with each other. God is the same way. He talks to us through Scripture, and we talk to Him through prayer. The more you talk to Him, the better you will get to know HIM. TRUST in Him to take care of your worries.

> **• How do you present your requests to God? How do these two verses encourage you to talk to Him throughout your day?**

> ```
> "Pray in the Spirit at all times and on every occasion . . ."
>                  Ephesians 6:18 (NLT)
> ```

> ```
>            " . . . pray without ceasing;"
>              1 Thessalonians 5:17 (NASB)
> ```

_____

_____

_____

_____

_____

_____

_____

_____

_____

_____

_____

Prayer: *Lord, thank You for this week of JOURNAL with ME. I pray to allow THANKSGIVING and PRAYER to diffuse the worry I have in my heart. I pray to find more time to spend with You! Thank You for this study and for spending time in Your Word. Teach me to trust You more. Teach me to give You my worry. Amen.*

CHALLENGE: How are you going to give your WORRY to God this week?

MEMORIZE: Go to page 63. Cut and copy the memory verse for this week. Remember to post it somewhere you can read it every day! When you are with each other, see if you can say it!

ART PROJECT: *The Joy Jar!*

Whenever you need to replace worry with JOY, drop your prayer request in the "Joy Jar." After a few weeks, read your prayers and see how God is FAITHFUL! Instructions below:

ART SUPPLIES:

- Container (soup can, glass jar, rice container, or plastic container)
- Glue (Elmers) . . . Mixed with a small amount of water
- Low-Temp Hot Glue Gun and Glue Sticks
- Foam Brush
- Fabric
- Ribbon, Wire, Yarn, Cording, Trim, Etc.
- Floral Wire (for handles)
- Scissors
- Embellishments (buttons, sequins, etc.)
- Drill
- Optional: 1 7/8 inch Punch (found at craft stores)
- Printer and Cardstock Paper
- Small Hole Punch
- Joy Jar Scripture Sheet: http://thouartexalted.com/bible-studies/girls-bible-studies/study-of-james-faith-into-action/art-instructions-videos/joy-jar-art-instructional-video/

ART INSTRUCTIONS:

How to: 1. Select and clean a container. 2. (Optional) Drill, or punch, two small holes in the opposite sides of the container. These holes will be used for handles. 3. Glue fabric onto the container using a mixture of water and glue (one tablespoon of glue to one/half teaspoon of water). 4. Choose fabric, cut to size, and wrap around your container. 5. Attach the handles using 15 inches of wire. 6. Using a hot (low-temp) glue gun, embellish the container with fabric, ribbon, trim, buttons, and more. 7. Attach memory verse for lesson three or use Scripture sheet listed in art supplies.

Write down your "worries" on pieces of paper, fold them up, and put them in your JOY JAR. A week, a month, or even a year later, take out one piece of paper and open it up. See how GOD uses the trials in your life to make your faith stronger and better.

For more pictures: Go to www.facebook.com/ThouArtExalted/**album/The Joy Jar**

Lesson FOUR: *Peace!*

- **Open with prayer and ask God to be with you in your time together.**

- **Take five minutes to discuss last week's *Journal with Me*. What did you learn about worry and giving it to the Lord?**

- **Start by reading Philippians 4:4-9.**

Opening DISCUSSION

In this lesson, we will study Philippians 4:7.

"And the peace of God, which transcends all understanding, will GUARD your hearts and your minds in Christ Jesus."

- **The first word we see in this verse is "AND." What is Paul trying to get us to remember? (Hint: Phil. 4:6)**

The word "AND" is very important in this passage. It is a conjunction used to connect two thoughts or, in this case, two sentences. This three letter word will be the glue that holds this lesson together.

- **Before reading the definition of PEACE, what do you think it means?**

"And the peace of God, which transcends all understanding, will GUARD your hearts and your minds in Christ Jesus."

Philippians 4:7

Definition: PEACE

freedom from disturbance; quiet and tranquility, free from anxiety or distress [1]

QUESTIONS TOGETHER

Here's a simple fill-in-the-blank quiz! Don't WORRY! This will NOT be graded.

- **What are the SIX actions God wants YOU to do to be able to experience His PEACE?**
  1. Rejoice _____.
  2. Let your _____ be evident to ALL.
  3. Do not _____ about ANYTHING.
  4. _____ about EVERYTHING.
  5. Be _____.
  6. Tell _____ what you need/ or present your requests to _____.

Great job! Paul tells us to rejoice ALWAYS, let your GENTLENESS be evident to all, do not WORRY about anything, PRAY about everything, be THANKFUL, and tell GOD what you need! For fun—see if you can put these concepts into a song. My girls and I put these verses to a very "catchy" Carrie Underwood song. Singing is a great memorization tool. Even though we are not the best singers, we will never forget God's Word or our time laughing together while creating this song!

Did you know God's most **foolish** thought doesn't even compare to the most **incredible** idea of man? Think of man's greatest accomplishment. Did you think of the i-phone, nuclear physics, or even open-heart surgery? **None of these** come close to the brilliance of God. Is that hard to believe? **Slowly read these different translations of 1 Corinthians 1:25.**

"This foolish plan of God is wiser than the wisest of human plans, and God's weakness is stronger than the greatest of human strength." (NLT)

". . . the foolishness of God is wiser than men, and the weakness of God is stronger than men." (NASB)

Philippians 4:7 says that God's PEACE surpasses anything we can understand. I don't know about you, but it makes me feel smarter that even a nuclear techno-wizard cannot wrap his mind around God's peace. God offers this peace to ALL of us when we choose to rejoice, be gentle, not to worry, pray with thanksgiving, and talk to Him. It's mind boggling!

"Then you will experience God's peace, which exceeds anything we can UNDERSTAND. His peace will guard your hearts and minds as you live in Christ Jesus."
Philippians 4:7 (NLT)

Scripture Search

Let's go back and look at our little, yet strong word, AND. *"**AND, the peace of God, which transcends all understanding, will guard your hearts and your minds in Christ Jesus.**"* Notice the verse does not say, "in just a minute, God will . . ." or "when He has enough time for you, God will . . ." or "maybe if you are good enough, God will . . ." This verse says, **"AND, GOD WILL . . ."** It's a promise that God keeps. God never lies. In fact, **He can't.**

- **Read Numbers 23:19 and Titus 1:2.**

    "God is not a man, so he does not lie. He is not human, so he does not change his mind. Has he ever spoken and failed to act? Has he ever promised and not carried it through?" Numbers 23:19 (NLT)

    ". . . God, who does not lie, promised . . . ." Titus 1:2

- **Peace is knowing the truth simply because God said it. How do these verses encourage you?**

- **2 Timothy 2:13 says,** *"If we are faithless, he remains faithful . . . ."*
Have you ever had the thought that God might turn His back on you after you have done something wrong? How does this truth encourage you?

God will ALWAYS remain faithful, even when we mess up.

- **• Read Psalm 103:12.**

    "As far as the east is from the west—that is how far
 he has removed our rebellious acts from himself." (God's Word)

- **• Rebellious acts are also called sin. How far has God forgiven us of our sin?**

_____

_____

- **• Read 1 John 1:9.**

    "If we confess our sins, he is faithful and just to forgive
 us our sins and to cleanse us from all unrighteousness." (ESV)

- **• What action must we take for God to forgive us? What is the result?**

_____

_____

_____

_____

In our last lesson, we talked about living in righteousness with God. 1 John 1:9 gives us the PROOF that we can! When we confess our sin before the Lord, He WILL forgive us and wash us from all the bad things that pollute our lives. God keeps His promises—even when we mess up. God is **always** there to provide His peace. Do you need a little peace today? Read this quote from Sarah Young:

"As you give yourself more and more to a life of constant communion with Me, you will find that you simply have no time for WORRY. Thus, you are freed to let my Spirit direct your steps, enabling you to walk along the path of PEACE." [2] Amen!

Main Lessons:

- God will give us HIS PEACE
    - —when we REJOICE
        - —when we are GENTLE IN SPIRIT
            - —when we are NOT WORRIED
                - —when we PRAY
                    - —when we are THANKFUL
                        - —when we communicate with GOD.

- God's peace goes BEYOND our human UNDERSTANDING.
- NOTHING can take away God's LOVE for us.

Prayer:

Thank YOU Lord, that we can experience Your peace when we TRUST in You. Peace is a PROMISE we can count on when we rejoice with thankful hearts and pray continuously! I pray for us to fully grasp the concept of being guarded in Your Peace. As we explore this verse, please open up our hearts and minds to know and follow Your Word in Christ Jesus. Be with us in our time together. Amen.

SNEAK PEEK:

This week, we will journal about:
- AND . . .
- The PEACE of GOD
- The PROTECTION of our HEARTS
- The PROTECTION of our MINDS
- The PRINCE OF PEACE~JESUS

"Then God's peace, which goes far beyond anything we can imagine, will GUARD your hearts and minds in union with the Messiah Jesus."

Philippians 4:7 (ISV)

• **Write down your Top TEN Favorite Movies or TV shows. Discuss the memories that go behind your answers.**

♥ MOMS

1. _____
2. _____
3. _____
4. _____
5. _____
6. _____
7. _____
8. _____
9. _____
10. _____

♥ DAUGHTERS

1. _____
2. _____
3. _____
4. _____
5. _____
6. _____
7. _____
8. _____
9. _____
10. _____

Prayer Requests: date: _____

We have already discussed that the PEACE of God goes BEYOND human understanding, AND that the PEACE of God is ALWAYS available. Today, we will discover more characteristics about God's peace.

• **Read Psalm 29:11 and Isaiah 26:3.**

> "The LORD will give strength to His people; The LORD will bless His people with peace." Psalm 29:11 (NASB)
>
> "You will keep in perfect peace all who trust in you, all whose thoughts are fixed on you!" Isaiah 26:3 (NLT)

• **Can you describe a difficult time in your life when you felt BLESSED with God's strength and peace?**

• **If you want to have this perfect peace, what do you have to do? (Isaiah 26:3) How are you going to do this?**

DAUGHTER

DAUGHTER

"And the peace of God, which transcends all understanding, will GUARD your hearts and your minds in Christ Jesus." Philippians 4:7

• **How would you define "to guard?"**

TO GUARD:
1. *watch over in order to protect or control* [3]
2. *to guard, protect by a military guard, either to prevent hostile invasion, or to keep the inhabitants of a besieged city from flight* [4]

• **Why do you think it is important to guard your HEART with the peace of God?**
In what ways do you think God's peace can guard your heart?

Our hearts are the center of our lives. Proverbs 16:22 says our hearts are the "wellspring of life." This simply means our heart is the fountain of life—the source of our joy. God desires that our source of joy come ONLY from Him. He knows that when we try to fill our lives with things other than Him, the fountain of our hearts becomes polluted with worry. This is another reason why He tells us to seek HIM FIRST before all things. He wants to be FIRST in our lives. This is why He makes it a top priority to GUARD our Hearts with His peace.

• **Describe a time when you ate too much—maybe too much cake! How did you feel?**

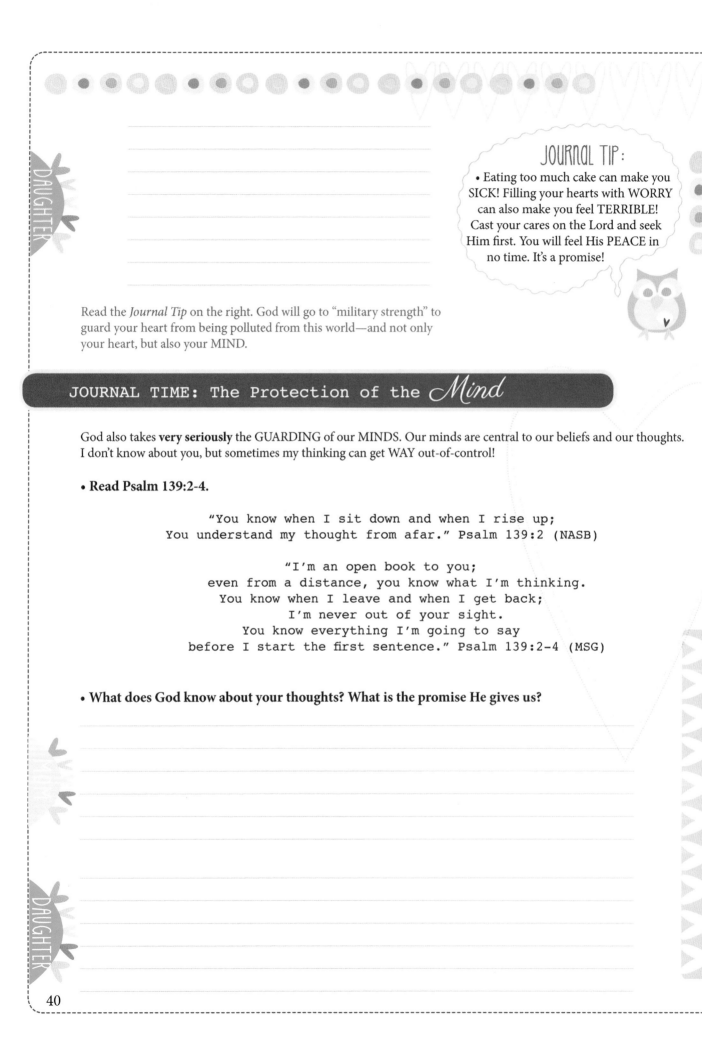

JOURNAL TIP:
• Eating too much cake can make you SICK! Filling your hearts with WORRY can also make you feel TERRIBLE! Cast your cares on the Lord and seek Him first. You will feel His PEACE in no time. It's a promise!

Read the *Journal Tip* on the right. God will go to "military strength" to guard your heart from being polluted from this world—and not only your heart, but also your MIND.

JOURNAL TIME: The Protection of the *Mind*

God also takes **very seriously** the GUARDING of our MINDS. Our minds are central to our beliefs and our thoughts. I don't know about you, but sometimes my thinking can get WAY out-of-control!

• **Read Psalm 139:2-4.**

> "You know when I sit down and when I rise up;
> You understand my thought from afar." Psalm 139:2 (NASB)
>
> "I'm an open book to you;
> even from a distance, you know what I'm thinking.
> You know when I leave and when I get back;
> I'm never out of your sight.
> You know everything I'm going to say
> before I start the first sentence." Psalm 139:2-4 (MSG)

• **What does God know about your thoughts? What is the promise He gives us?**

• Read 2 Corinthians 10:5.

> "... we take captive every thought to make it obedient to Christ."

• **Why do you think it's important to give EVERY thought to Christ? Where can our thinking lead us if our thoughts are not right?**

_____

_____

_____

_____

_____

_____

_____

_____

_____

_____

_____

_____

_____

_____

We must remember that GOD is protecting our hearts and our minds in **His PEACE**—a peace that goes beyond our human understanding. This is made possible when we rejoice in Him, pray continuously, praise Him with THANKSGIVING, and GIVE Him our cares and worries! He's GOD. If He created YOU, don't you think He can handle your concerns for the day? Let's protect our MINDS today with the power of HIS PEACE!

JOURNAL TIME: The Prince of Peace – _Jesus!_

The last part of our verse for this lesson all boils down to **Jesus, the Prince of Peace**. The PEACE of GOD guards our hearts, but it is IN Jesus that this is ABLE to happen. Because Jesus made us right with God through the sacrifice of His perfect life for us, we are now able to experience God's perfect peace.

• Read John 16:33.

> "I have told you these things, so that in me you may have peace. In this world you will have trouble. But take heart! I have overcome the world." John 16:33

• **How did Jesus overcome the world?**

_____

_____

_____

_____

And the peace of God, which transcends all understanding, will GUARD your _hearts and your minds_ in _Christ Jesus."_

Philippians 4:7

• Read the New Living Translation of John 14:27.

> "I am leaving you with a gift--peace of mind and heart. And the peace I give is a gift the world cannot give. So don't be troubled or afraid." John 14:27

• What are the two "GIFTS" Christ leaves with us? Do they sound familiar? Why do you think Jesus tells us not to be afraid?

• Of what do you tend to be afraid? How can the peace of God be a "gift" to your fears?

Jesus isn't called the Prince of Peace without reason! He came to take away your fears and replace them with an abundant life in Him. AND . . . God's peace WILL guard your hearts and minds IN Jesus. This is a promise we can REST in today. Great job on this lesson. I pray that by looking into all these SCRIPTURES, you are grasping HOW much God loves you!

Prayer: *Lord, thank You for this lesson in Journal with Me. Your Peace that surpasses understanding is my blessing and my strength. Teach me to let go of my worry and to be washed with Your peace. I pray You will protect my heart and my mind from the things of this world. Help me to seek YOU first in all things and know my rest is in Jesus. Thank You for the opportunity to study Your Word with one I dearly love. I pray You would always remain in the center of our friendship. We both love You! Amen.*

CHALLENGE: Look for ways God will GUARD your heart and your mind when you rejoice, pray with thankful and gentle hearts, and not worry. Invite Him into a friendship with you.

MEMORIZE: Go to page 63. Cut and copy the memory verse for this week. Remember to post it somewhere you can read it every day! When you are with each other, see if you can say it!

ART PROJECT: *Heart Pencils!*

This HEART ART will remind you that IN Jesus, you will always have the peace of GOD.

Heart Pencils!

ART SUPPLIES:

- Colorful Pencils
- Pipe Cleaners

ART INSTRUCTIONS:

How to: This project could not get any easier. It's fast, fun, and a great little gift!
1. Buy a pack of colorful pencils.
2. Take a pipe cleaner and wrap the bottom of one end two times around the eraser side of your pencil.
3. Bringing the pipe cleaner straight up, form a heart shape. Secure the open end back onto the pencil. Voila!

IDEA! Make a dozen or more pencils and give them to your class, family, Sunday school teachers, or friends. You can also copy the memory verse and attach it to your pencil!

For a video instruction: Go to http://thouartexalted.com/valentines-day-pencils/

• **Open with prayer and ask God to be with you in your time together.**

• **Take five minutes to discuss last week's *Journal with Me*. What did you learn about God's peace? How can it guard your heart and your mind in Christ Jesus?**

• **Start by reading Philippians 4:4-9.**

"Finally, brothers and sisters, whatever is whatever is whatever is whatever is whatever is whatever is -- if anything is excellent or praiseworthy -think about such things."
Philippians 4:8

Opening DISCUSSION

In this lesson, we will study Philippians 4:8.

"Finally, brothers and sisters, whatever is true, whatever is noble, whatever is right, whatever is pure, whatever is lovely, whatever is admirable--if anything is excellent or praiseworthy--THINK about such things."

• **The first word we see in this verse is "finally." What do you think Paul is trying to tell us?**

_____

_____

Definition: THINK

to direct one's mind toward someone or something; to use one's mind actively to form connected ideas . . . [1]

Finally ~ Paul is closing up the book of Philippians with some important information. In his closing remarks, he is essentially saying, "Listen up! I've got some good advice for REAL CHRISTIAN LIVING." I think we better listen!

• **Before reading the definition of THINK, how would you define it?**

_____

_____

QUESTIONS TOGETHER

In our final two lessons, Paul will sum up our time together by telling us TWO THINGS:

1. **Think about** what is TRUE, NOBLE, RIGHT, PURE, LOVELY, ADMIRABLE, EXCELLENT AND PRAISEWORTHY; and

2. Put THESE into practice!

Paul tells us to rejoice in the Lord, **always**. He reminds us that our gentle nature can be a godly example of Christian living. Paul tells us to not worry about this life, but instead be thankful and give God our concerns. He also promises us that God's PEACE will protect our hearts and our minds in Christ. Today, he is telling us to FILL our hearts with **good things**. Paul knows that what we THINK will eventually trickle down into our heart and into our actions—whether good or bad. When we THINK positive and good things, goodness flows out of our hearts. When our minds are filled with excellence, our speech and actions will pour out blessings.

• **What fills your heart today that will pour over into your speech and actions?**
(Remember, critical thoughts have the same effect!)

_____

_____

Did you know your Mom **knows** when you are having a good day and when you are having a bad day? She can detect it from the way you are acting and from the words you are saying. Your Mom knows your heart. God does, too. He knows **everything** flows from it. He knows that what we hold in our hearts will eventually come right out of our mouths and into our actions. If you are sad, your feelings will spill out. If you are anxious, worry surfaces. If you are angry, hurtful words will hurt others. The same is true with being joyful. Circumstances may not be perfect, but if you are living in faith, joy flows into blessings for all those around you.

- **Read Proverbs 4:23 (inset) and Matthew 15:18 below.**

> "But what comes out of the mouth
> comes from the heart." (HCSB)

Paul is teaching us an amazing lesson! Take a moment to think about this. What is in your heart, right now, that could spill over into your speech? An unguarded heart is a dangerous thing! This is why God goes to great lengths to teach us how to **guard** it. Paul encourages us to think about what is true, noble, right, pure, lovely, admirable, excellent, and praiseworthy because when we center our minds on these, we fill our hearts with the goodness of God that can overflow to others.

"Above ALL else,
guard your
heart,
for everything
you do flows
from it."
Proverbs 4:23

Scripture Search

"Think about such things . . ." Paul knows we often get wrapped up in **negative thinking**. Our thoughts can spiral downward quicker than my dog can eat the peanut butter toast off of my kitchen counter. Think about your thoughts JUST this morning. Were any of them negative? Okay, I'll be the first to confess. I have already wished my hair would have cooperated, my children would have made their own lunches, and that I would find time to exercise! What has filled my heart? Hmmmm, let's see. How about complaining? YUCK. I want to be filled with excellence and truth. Let's try this exercise together and see the ways in which we can change our negative thoughts into positive ones.

- *Negative THOUGHTS:*

My hair is a mess! I hate the way it looks today.

- *Positive THOUGHTS:*
Think about what is true, noble, right, pure, lovely, admirable, excellent, and praiseworthy.

Thank You, Lord, that I have hair. Show me ways to use a pony-tail holder, hair spray, and bobby-pins!

The qualities Paul is telling us to THINK about will help us to keep our FOCUS on God alone. This way of biblical thinking will fill our hearts with godly character instead of with the attitudes of the world. Why is this important? As God's children, we have a responsibility to reflect His nature and draw others to faith in Christ. Let's review why this is true.

> **• Read 1 John 4:19 and Ephesians 2:8-10.**

> "We love because he first loved us." 1 John 4:19

"For it is by grace you have been saved, through faith—and this is not from yourselves, it is the GIFT of God—not by works, so that no one can boast. For we are God's handiwork, created in Christ Jesus to do good works, which God prepared in advance for us to do." Ephesians 2:8-10

> **• What GIFTS has God given to you?** (Think about your family, your talents, or even your smile!)

_____

_____

_____

> **• According to Ephesians 2:8-10, why were you created?**

_____

_____

_____

We must always remember that having a personal relationship with God is only possible through Jesus Christ. It is a **GIFT.** Faith in Christ is possible not because we are good, but because GOD is GOOD and LOVED us **first**. God creates each of us with a purpose on this earth. *The Message* says, *"He creates each of us by Christ Jesus to join him in the work he does, the good work he has gotten ready for us to do, work we had better be doing"* (Ephesians 2:10).

> **• What talents and gifts has God given you that you "better be doing?"**

_____

_____

_____

We are not created to sit around and think negative thoughts. We are created to JOIN Jesus in the work He is doing! Because God loved us first and gave us the GIFT of Jesus, let us use our talents and THOUGHTS to glorify HIM.

Main Lessons:

- Think about what is TRUE, NOBLE, RIGHT, PURE, LOVELY, ADMIRABLE, EXCELLENT, AND PRAISEWORTHY.
- Our actions and speech flow from the heart.
- God loved us FIRST and has given us GIFTS to use for His glory.

Prayer: ♥

Lord, help us to think about what is positive and avoid the negative. Place in our HEARTS godly thinking that will overflow with YOUR Words. Remind us that YOU loved us first and gave us special gifts and talents to use so we may glorify YOU! Thank you for this time together. Amen.

"Finally, brethren, whatever things are true, whatever things are noble, whatever things are just, whatever things are pure, whatever things are lovely, whatever things are of good report, if there is any virtue and if there is anything praiseworthy— meditate on these things."

Philippians 4:8 (NKJV)

• Write down your Top TEN Favorite Places to VISIT. Discuss why these are special.

♥ MOMS

1. _____
2. _____
3. _____
4. _____
5. _____
6. _____
7. _____
8. _____
9. _____
10. _____

♥ DAUGHTERS

1. _____
2. _____
3. _____
4. _____
5. _____
6. _____
7. _____
8. _____
9. _____
10. _____

Prayer Requests: date: _____

In each lesson, we will learn about TWO of the characteristics Paul wants us to THINK about. Today, we will begin with **TRUE** and **NOBLE**.

Definition: TRUE

being in accordance with the actual state or conditions, sincere, not deceitful, loving the truth, speaking the truth, truthful [2]

• **Look at the definition of TRUE. Why is it important to think about what is true? What is the opposite of TRUTH?**

• **Read the following verses.**

"For the word of the Lord is right and TRUE;
he is faithful in all he does." Psalm 33:4

"But the Lord is the TRUE God;
he is the living God, the eternal King." Jeremiah 10:10

"Yet you are near, Lord,
and all your commands are TRUE." Psalm 119:151

• **From these verses, what is TRUE about God? Why should we think about this TRUTH?**

• **Read the definition of NOBLE. Why is it important to think about noble things? What is the opposite of being NOBLE?**

JOURNAL TIME: *Right and Pure*

• **Read the definition of RIGHT. Why do you think it's important to keep focused on what is right? What is the opposite of RIGHT?**

• **Read the definition of PURE. Why do you think it's important to focus upon what is PURE? What is the opposite of PURE?**

_____
_____
_____
_____
_____

JOURNAL TIME: *Lovely and Admirable*

• **Read the definition of LOVELY and ADMIRABLE. What do you think are their opposites?**

_____
_____
_____
_____
_____
_____
_____

> **Definition:** LOVELY
> charming or exquisitely beautiful, having beauty that appeals to the heart or mind, delightful, of a great moral or spiritual beauty, acceptable, pleasing [6]
>
> **Definition:** ADMIRABLE
> worthy of admiration, excellent, first-rate [7]

I believe Paul is telling us we should admire what is lovely. I know God wants us to FILL our hearts with EVERYTHING that is first-rate and exquisitely beautiful. When our minds are focused on this kind of beauty, our hearts will overflow with His love. How awesome!

• **When you think of filling up your heart with this first-rate, exquisite beauty, what comes to your mind? How do these things overflow into your speech and actions?**

_____
_____
_____
_____
_____
_____
_____
_____
_____

• **Read the definition of EXCELLENT and PRAISEWORTHY. Why is it important to think about these words? What are their opposite meanings?**

Definition: EXCELLENT
possessing outstanding quality or superior merit, remarkably good, extraordinary [8]

Definition: PRAISEWORTHY
desiring of praise [9]

After looking closely at these virtues, do you have a better idea why GOD wants to fill our hearts with these thoughts? We need to use these godly characteristics to protect our hearts. It's almost like **"Spiritual Saran Wrap™!"** Picture yourself wrapping your heart in this. The packing would say: "Wrap your thoughts in SPIRITUAL SARAN WRAP™. It will keep your mind fresh and free from ugly, false, and critical judgement. **Spiritual Saran Wrap™** seals your heart in truth, purity, loveliness, excellence, and praise! This product comes with a full, money-back guarantee. No limited time offer. It's available everyday—for free!"

• **How are you going to use your "Spiritual Saran Wrap™" today?**

CHALLENGE : Look for ways to think about what is true, noble, right, pure, lovely, admirable, excellent, and praiseworthy.

MEMORIZE : Go to page 63. Cut and copy the memory verse for this week. Remember to post it somewhere you can read it every day! When you are with each other, see if you can recite it!

SERVICE PROJECT : Write a letter to someone you admire who guards their hearts with the godly qualities Paul admonishes. Copy this card and send the letter today!

Cut Here

Spiritual SARAN WRAP *Stationery*

"*Finally*, brothers and sisters, whatever is
whatever is
whatever is
whatever is
whatever is
whatever is   --
if anything is
excellent or praiseworthy
-think about such things."
Philippians 4:8

Lesson SIX: *Practice!*

• **Open with prayer and ask God to be with you in your time together.**

• **Take five minutes to discuss last week's *Journal with Me*. What did you learn from thoughts that are true, noble, right, lovely, admirable, excellent, and praiseworthy? How did your new thinking overflow into your speech and actions?**

• **Start by reading Philippians 4:4-9.**

Opening DISCUSSION

After last week's lesson, I picked up my children from school and told them about **Spiritual Saran Wrap** ™. How TRUE it is that what we say reflects what is in our hearts. It's a good lesson for ALL of us. I pray we would fill our hearts with goodness so we can speak words of love, joy, and peace!

Can you believe this is our last lesson in *Journal with Me*? Let's read Philippians 4:9.

> *"Whatever you have learned or received or heard from me, or seen in me--put it into practice. And the God of peace will be with you."*

Paul is telling the Christians in Philippi to follow his example. Paul was a warrior for Christ and risked his life many times to tell people the truth about Jesus.

• **What are the four actions Paul is telling us to remember and "put into practice?"** (Philippians 4:9)

• **"Whatever you have_____ or _____ or or _____ . . . put into PRACTICE"** (Philippians 4:8).

• **Before reading the definition of PRACTICE, what do you think it means?**

_____

"Whatever you have learned or received or heard from me, or seen in me--put it into practice. And the God of peace will be with you." Philippians 4:8

Definition: PRACTICE
rehearse, run through, go over/through, work on/at; polish, perfect, prepare, carry out[1]

QUESTIONS TOGETHER

It is important to remember that Paul is in prison while writing this letter to the Philippian church. They, unlike us, knew Paul personally and were very familiar with his teachings, his mission trips, his persecutions, and his ministry. He is reminding them to carry out this Christian life with faith and trust in God's promises.

• **What have you learned, received, heard, or seen from these six verses in Philippians that you can "put into practice?"**

_____

_____

_____

Did you know Paul is attributed with writing fourteen books in the Bible? He wrote Romans, 1 & 2 Corinthians, Galatians, Ephesians, Philippians, Colossians, 1 & 2 Thessalonians, 1 & 2 Timothy, Titus, Philemon, and some theologians speculate Hebrews. Unlike the Philippians, we do not KNOW Paul personally, but we can follow his example through reading these books, called epistles. If you want to know how to "put into practice" what these early believers learned, received, heard, or saw—read these books in the Bible!

"Keep putting into practice all you learned and received from me—everything you heard from me and saw me doing. Then the God of peace will be with you.

Philippians 4:8 (NLT)

Scripture Search

Paul's original name was Saul. He was a Jewish Pharisee who strongly opposed the truth that Jesus was the Son of God—the Messiah. In fact, he was so intent on silencing Christianity, he *"began to destroy the church. Going from house to house, he dragged off men and women and put them in prison"* (Acts 8:3). This certainly is NOT the example he is telling us to follow in Philippians 4:9, nor is this the Paul we know and admire. Jesus had a one-on-one meeting with Saul that changed his heart completely.

- **Read Acts 9:1-19.**

- **Why was Saul going to Damascus? (verse 2)**

- **Why did Saul fall to the ground? What did he SEE and HEAR? (verses 3-5)**

- **Why would Ananias have been afraid to go to Saul? (verses 13-14)**

- **What was the Lord's response to Ananias? (verses 15-16)**

I love that God refers to Paul as His "chosen instrument" to carry out His name before the Gentiles. Today, Paul's message is still being carried into the world, and WE are benefiting from his obedience to follow Christ. Remember what "practice" means? One of the definitions is "to carry out!" Paul was PRACTICING what he was PREACHING. Maybe that's where we get the phrase "practice what you preach."

> **• In our last lesson, we read Ephesians 2:10. Let's read this verse again in the New American Standard Version.**

> *"For we are His workmanship, created in Christ Jesus for good works, which God prepared beforehand so that we would walk in them." Ephesians 2:8-10*

> **• What do you think "workmanship" means?**

_____

_____

_____

Workmanship comes from the greek word ***poiema***.[2] Does this word look familiar to you? YES! It's where we get the english word, POEM. We are God's poem—how cool is that? Our lives are written by the hand of God to rejoice in Him always, to have gentle spirits, to not worry, pray, and be thankful. We are written with the pen of grace and mercy by a loving Father who protects our hearts and our minds through His peace perfected in Jesus. Each day, we are living out a stanza of our poem. Our life pages reflect the unique gifts and talents we use to glorify the King of Kings. And when others read our poem, they see the reflection of Christ in us.

• Read Ephesians 5:1 in the New Living Translation.

`"Imitate God, therefore, in everything you do, because you are his dear children."`

Paul is telling us that whatever we have learned, received, heard, or seen from the teachings of the Bible, put into practice. He also tells us in this passage that we are to be **imitators** of God in ALL that we do. Why? Because we are His masterpiece, His creation, His children, and His poem.

How are you going to "practice" and carry out the unique poem God has written for you?

_____

_____

Main Lessons:

- Put Biblical teachings into practice.
- Jesus changed Saul's life so he became a "chosen instrument."
- We are God's poem chosen to imitate Christ.

Prayer: ♥

Thank You for Journal with Me! Thank You also for our mornings together learning more about You. Help us to take what we have learned, received, heard, and seen, "to heart." We pray others will see the beautiful poem You have written for us. We pray we can be imitators of who You are because we are Your children. Yes, Lord, each of us is Your masterpiece. Identify in us the gifts You have given to us so we can be Your chosen instrument. We pray the song of our lives will be a lovely melody with which You alone are pleased. Use our poems Lord, to serve You and to carry out Your message to those around us. We love You. Amen.

SNEAK PEEK:

This week, we will journal about:
- Chosen Instruments
- What have you Learned?
- What have you Received?
- What have you Heard?
- What have you Seen?

"Put into practice what you learned from me, what you heard and saw and realized. Do that, and God, who makes everything work together, will work you into his most excellent harmonies."

Philippians 4:9 (NKJV)

• Write down your Top TEN Favorite Songs. Discuss why these songs have a special memory.

♥ MOMS

1. _____
2. _____
3. _____
4. _____
5. _____
6. _____
7. _____
8. _____
9. _____
10. _____

♥ DAUGHTERS

1. _____
2. _____
3. _____
4. _____
5. _____
6. _____
7. _____
8. _____
9. _____
10. _____

Prayer Requests: date: _____

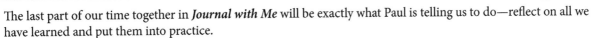

The last part of our time together in *Journal with Me* will be exactly what Paul is telling us to do—reflect on all we have learned and put them into practice.

• **Look through your notes. Write down the new things you learned from studying Philippians 4:4-9.**

_____

_____

_____

_____

_____

_____

_____

_____

_____

_____

_____

_____

_____

_____

_____

_____

_____

_____

• **Read Proverbs 1:7 from *The Message*.**

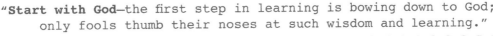

"**Start with God**—the first step in learning is bowing down to God;
only fools thumb their noses at such wisdom and learning."

• **What can we LEARN about "LEARNING" from this verse?**

_____

_____

_____

_____

_____

_____

_____

_____

To receive something, you have to take it and make it yours. For example, if you receive mail, you open it, read it, and take action, if needed. If someone gives you a gift, you take it, unwrap it, and it becomes a blessing to you.

- **What have you received from your time together? How has this study been a blessing to you?**

_____
_____
_____
_____
_____
_____
_____
_____
_____
_____
_____
_____
_____
_____
_____
_____
_____
_____

JOURNAL TIME: *What have you Heard?*

Begin today by reading Luke 11:28, James 1:22, and John 13:17.

> "Jesus replied, "But even more blessed are all who hear the word of God and put it into practice." Luke 11:28 (NLT)
>
> "Do not merely listen to the word, and so deceive yourselves. DO what it says." James 1:22
>
> "Now that you KNOW these things, you will be BLESSED if you DO them." John 13:17

- **What does Jesus say at the end of Luke 11:28? Why does this sound familiar?**

_____
_____
_____

• According to these verses, why do you think we are "even more blessed" when we hear the Word and DO what it says?

JOURNAL TIME: *What have you Seen?*

Paul says, "Whatever . . . you have SEEN in me, put into practice and the peace of God will be with you" (Philippians 4:9). I can only imagine the many people in your life who admire you because they have SEEN the way you live out your life as an example of Christ. When we live our lives for the Lord, others can see—even when we are not aware they are watching!

• Who have you watched live the example of following Christ? What have you SEEN that makes you know the peace of God is with them? How will you put into practice what you have seen?

For our final question, read Philippians 4:9 from *The Message*.

"Put into practice what you learned from me,

what you heard and saw and realized.

Do that, and God, who makes everything work together, will work you into his most excellent harmonies.

We studied about the peace of God in lesson four. Today, we learn that when we are wrapped in God's peace, our lives are working into "His most excellent harmonies!" Can you hear the orchestra starting to play? Just as we SEE the example of Christ in others, others see the example of Christ in us. When we live in the harmony of God's plan for our lives, people SEE the peace of God in us.

• **Think about your life right now and what you are going through. How will you practice what you have learned in studying Philippians 4:4-9 so others will SEE God's peace in your life and HEAR His most excellent harmony?**

Prayer: *Lord, thank You for this time together in Journal with Me. Thank You for the special relationship You have built between the two of us. We pray to rejoice in You, always, regardless of the circumstances we are going through. YOU alone are our object of JOY! We pray to have gentle spirits that give EVIDENCE of Your amazing and gracious love. We pray not to WORRY, but with THANKSGIVING present our requests to YOU. We ask that Your PEACE guard our HEARTS and MINDS in Christ, and that we will only think about that which is true, noble, right, pure, lovely, admirable, excellent, and praiseworthy. We also pray we would be Your most excellent melody. May our lives reflect the beautiful poem You have written uniquely for us. Whatever we have learned from this study, we pray we can put it into practice. We praise You and lift Your name on High! Amen*

CHALLENGE: Listen for the tune God has put into your heart! What can you "put into practice" that you have learned, received, heard, or seen from this study?

MEMORIZE: Go to page 63. Cut and copy the memory verse for this week. Remember to post it somewhere you can read it every day! When you are with each other, see if you can recite it.

ART PROJECT: *Sing a Song of Peace!* Follow the directions to paint and collage a beautiful reminder that we are to "put into practice" what we have learned, received, heard, and seen!

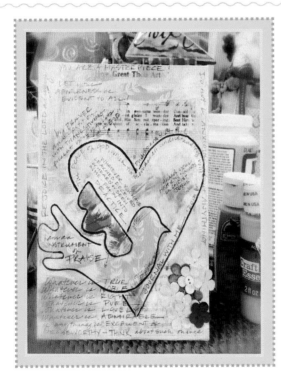

Sing a song of *Peace*

ART SUPPLIES:

• 5 x 7 canvas (bigger is good too)
• Sheet music (google free downloads of *How Great Thou Art*)
• Picture of a bird (download template: http://thouartexalted.com/bible-studies/girls-bible-studies/journal-with-me-mother-and-daughter-devotional-study/)
• Acrylic Paint (assorted colors)
• Paint Brush
• Modge Podge
• Foam Brush-1 inch brush
• Black Sharpie, Pencil
• Embellishments (flowers, buttons, glitter . . .)

ART INSTRUCTIONS:

How to: 1. Print out sheet music and cut to fit your 5 x 7 canvas. Using your foam brush, glue the sheet music onto your canvas using Modge Podge. Tip: Using a credit card, scrape over your canvas to get the "air bubbles" out. 2. Using bird and heart template (link written above), cut it out and trace onto scrapbooking paper. Cut out the scrapbooking paper, and glue it on top of your sheet music. 3. Using brisk strokes, paint color on top of your canvas. Be careful to leave some of the sheet music exposed. I like to mix my color with white using a "dry" brush. Once canvas is dry, outline your bird and heart in black sharpie (This is an optional step. You might like your canvas without the black outline.) 4. Using a pencil, write down the verses that meant most to you during your study together. 5. Embellish your canvas with paper flowers, buttons, or glitter. Have FUN with this project. This art will remind you of your time together!

NOTES:

Lesson One: REJOICE

1. Definition of rejoice: http://www.bluetetterbible.org/lang/lexicon/lexicon cfm?Strongs=G5463&t=KJV, http://www.thefreedictionary.com/rejoice.
2. Excerpt from *Paul's Roman Imprisonment*, http://www.christianinconnect.com/bkgdpriepi.htm.
3. Henri J.M. Nouwen, *Show Me the Way, Daily Lenten Readings*, The Crossroad Publishing Company, 1994, pg. 8.
4. Norman Vincent Peale, http://thinkexist.com/quotation/repetition_of_the_same_thought_or_physical_action/257792.html.

Lesson Two: GENTLENESS

1. Definition of gentleness: http://www.thefreedictionary.com/Gentleness, http://www.biblestudytools.com/dictionary/gentleness/.
2. Definition of evidence: Mac Dictionary.
3. Definition of leprosy: Mac Dictionary.

Lesson Three: PRAYER

1. Definition of worry: Mac Dictionary.
2. Quote from Corrie Ten Boom, http://www.goodreads.com/work/quotes/3616670-clippings-from-my-notebook.
3. Definition of thankful: Mac Dictionary.

Lesson Four: PEACE

1. Definition of peace: Mac Dictionary.
2. Sarah Young, *Jesus Calling*, (Nashville, Tennessee, Thomas Nelson Publishing, ©2004), May 1, pg. 128.
3. Definition of guard: Mac Dictionary.
4. Definition of guard: http://www.bluetetterbible.org/lang/lexicon/lexicon.cfm?Strongs=G5432&t=KJV.

Lesson Five: THINK

1. Definition of think: Mac Dictionary.
2. Definition of true: http://www.dictionary.com, and http://www.bluetetterbible.org/lang/lexicon/lexicon cfm?Strongs=G227&t=KJV.
3. Definition of noble: http://www.dictionary.com, and http://www.bluetetterbible.org/lang/lexicon/lexicon cfm?Strongs=G227&t=KJV.
4. Definition of right: http://www.dictionary.com, and http://www.bluetetterbible.org/lang/lexicon/lexicon cfm?Strongs=G227&t=KJV.
5. Definition of pure: http://www.dictionary.com, and http://www.bluetetterbible.org/lang/lexicon/lexicon cfm?Strongs=G227&t=KJV.
6. Definition of lovely: http://www.dictionary.com, and http://www.bluetetterbible.org/lang/lexicon/lexicon cfm?Strongs=G227&t=KJV.
8. Definition of excellent: http://www.dictionary.com, and http://www.bluetetterbible.org/lang/lexicon/lexicon cfm?Strongs=G227&t=KJV.
9. Definition of praiseworthy: http://www.dictionary.com, and http://www.bluetetterbible.org/lang/lexicon/lexicon cfm?Strongs=G227&t=KJV.

Lesson Six: PRATICE

1. Definition of practice: Mac Dictionary.
2. Poiema: http://www.biblestudytools.com/lexicons/greek/nas/poiema.html.

> God *all* day,
> EVERY DAY. I mean,
> in HIM!"
> Philippians 4:4(MSG)

Annie Pajcic lives in Jacksonville, Florida with her husband and four children. Using her background in youth ministry, dance, and graphic design, she started ThouArtExalted in 2007. ThouArtExalted is a ministry using God's Word with the combination of art. When she doesn't have paint on her hands, she is writing and designing Bible studies, picking up kids, cooking, or feeding the chickens. Visit her website at **www.thouartexalted.com** for art ideas, Bible studies, speaking engagements, service projects, and art blogotionals. Check out **www.facebook.com/ThouArtExalted** to see pictures of art projects in progress!

Memory *Verses*

• Color copy and cut out the verses to MEMORIZE each week!
(Idea: Laminate for extra durability)

"Rejoice in the Lord,
I will say it again!

Philippians 4:4

"Let your gentleness
be evident to ALL.
THE *Lord is near."*
Philippians 4:5

"Do not be *anxious* about
anything, but in everything,
by *prayer* and *petition*,
with THANKSGIVING, present
your requests to *God."*
Philippians 4:6

"And the *peace* of
God, which TRANSCENDS
all understanding, will
guard your *hearts* and
your *minds* in
CHRIST JESUS."
Philippians 4:7

"Finally, brothers, whatever is *true*,
whatever is *noble*, whatever is RIGHT,
whatever is *pure*, whatever is LOVELY,
whatever is   --if anything
is **excellent** or **praiseworthy**
--think about such things.
Philippians 4:8

"Whatever you have learned or
received or heard *from me, or*
seen *in me--put it into*
practice. And the God of peace
will be with you."
Philippians 4:9

MEMORY TIP:
• Say the verse OUT LOUD
as many times as
you can. • Use it in conversation.
• Write it down.

63

James: One Year Curriculum for PRETEEN Girls and Boys

James: *Following God's Road Signs* is a 27-week Bible study on the book of James for middle school girls and boys. It is written to encourage and deepen your faith when life isn't quite so easy. But God is on your side and gives you INSTRUCTIONS for how to navigate—even when you choose to drive your OWN way often finding yourself on dead-end streets. The book of James is a road map guiding you in the right direction. *Following God's Road Signs* teaches you to put your FAITH INTO ACTION by stopping, looking at God's map, and asking HIM for directions. This study is great for Youth Groups, Small Groups, and Homeschool Groups.

What You Get:
- Study The Book Of James Verse-By-Verse In A Fun, Creative & Preteen-Friendly Way
- 27 Exciting Bible Lessons
- Creative Art Projects
- Dig-Deep Discussion Questions
- Lessons Come In a **Digital PDF** Format For Easy Sharing

Creative Art Projects

Planted: Women's Study
Sit, Stand, and Walk with Jesus

PLANTED is a ten-week **women's Bible study** on Psalm 1:1-3. The study will teach you how to give up control and let God PLANT you where you need to be—so you can grow UP into the strong tree described in Psalm 1:2-3. When your roots are deeply PLANTED into the fellowship, the love, the grace, and the Word of God, you can't help but become a beautiful strong tree with purpose. Your leaf will not wither under the stresses and storms of life, your fruit will be abundant, and your lives will prosper! It's a promise on which you can stand.

Made in the USA
Columbia, SC
28 August 2018